My Blob Feelings Workbook is accompanied by a number of printable online materials, designed to ensure this resource best supports your professional needs.

Go to https://resourcecentre.routledge.com/speechmark and click on the cover of this book.

Answer the question prompt using your copy of the book to gain access to the online content.

T0373485

MY BLOB FEELINGS WORKBOOK

My Blob Feelings Workbook provides the reader with a series of unique visual reflective exercises that help to reveal one's own emotional portrait. Using a combination of Blob characters and open questions, the reader can gradually build up an image of themselves across a wide range of 'who I am' subjects and real-life scenarios.

Packed with well-loved blob illustrations, this book includes a wealth of downloadable pages and will enable the individual to 'draw' a picture of themselves emotionally through the series of exercises. Sections covered include:

- My Charts
- My Feeling Scales
- My Scenarios
- Myself Scales

Best used as a personal toolkit for self-awareness, this book is also a rich resource for professionals working in the field of feelings to use with their own clients. It is suitable for all ages from secondary school upwards and ideal for individuals, couples, groups and all who wish to go deeper in understanding their emotional strengths and areas for development.

Pip Wilson is the author of over 50 books and the famous Blob Tree tools, which can open the hardest heart, and are able to open up meaningful communication in all cultures and contexts.

Ian Long is an illustrator who has worked with Pip all of his adult life, drawing, creating and visualising ideas that they have imagined together since the early 1980s. He has been a youth and pastoral worker in Gloucestershire, a primary school teacher in West Sussex and Hampshire, a carer for his father who suffered with Alzheimer's and is now working full-time on books.

Blobs

Blobs are delightful characters (without gender or age) that help facilitate and stimulate meaningful discussions about difficult issues or situations. Individuals or groups can start discussions by identifying themselves, or others, with an individual or group of blobs whose actions or feelings represent their own.

The series includes a range of activities, books and posters, suitable for all ages.

Authors: Pip Wilson and Ian Long

Titles in this series include:

My Blob Feelings Workbook: A Toolkit for Exploring Emotions!

Blob Bullying

The Blob Guide to Children's Human Rights

The Big Book of Blobs (2nd edition)

The Big Book of Blob Trees (2nd edition)

The Big Book of Blob Feelings

The Big Book of Blob Feelings 2

The Blob Anger Book

Feelings Blob Cards

Emotions Blob Cards

Anger Blob Cards

Bereavement Blob Cards

Behaviour Blob Cards

Family Blob Cards

Teenage Life Blob Cards

Blob School

The Blob Visual Emotional Thesaurus

Giant Blob Tree Poster

Blob Feelings Ball

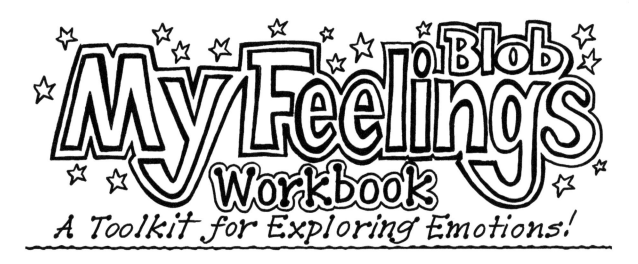

Pip Wilson + Ian Long

MY BLOB FEELINGS WORKBOOK

A TOOLKIT FOR EXPLORING EMOTIONS!

Pip Wilson and Ian Long

Routledge
Taylor & Francis Group

LONDON AND NEW YORK

Designed cover image: Ian Long

First published 2024
by Routledge
4 Park Square, Milton Park, Abingdon, Oxon OX14 4RN

and by Routledge
605 Third Avenue, New York, NY 10158

Routledge is an imprint of the Taylor & Francis Group, an informa business

© 2024 Pip Wilson and Ian Long

The right of Pip Wilson and Ian Long to be identified as authors of this work has been asserted in accordance with sections 77 and 78 of the Copyright, Designs and Patents Act 1988.

All rights reserved. The purchase of this copyright material confers the right on the purchasing institution to photocopy or download pages which bear the support material icon and a copyright line at the bottom of the page. No other parts of this book may be reprinted or reproduced or utilised in any form or by any electronic, mechanical, or other means, now known or hereafter invented, including photocopying and recording, or in any information storage or retrieval system, without permission in writing from the publishers.

Trademark notice: Product or corporate names may be trademarks or registered trademarks, and are used only for identification and explanation without intent to infringe.

British Library Cataloguing-in-Publication Data
A catalogue record for this book is available from the British Library

ISBN: 978-1-032-59852-9 (hbk)
ISBN: 978-1-032-59844-4 (pbk)
ISBN: 978-1-003-45655-1 (ebk)

DOI: 10.4324/9781003456551

Typeset in Helvetica
by Apex CoVantage, LLC

Access the Support Material: https://resourcecentre.routledge.com/speechmark

This book is dedicated to Pip Wilson, my brother, who helped me to become a beautiful human person. – Ian Long

Contents

Introduction

The Blob books series have been previously designed around discussion materials, usually between two people or small groups. This book is different. Its starting point is for the reader. The more that we know ourselves, understanding our feelings and their patterns, the more that we can help others to perceive and self-regulate their own. Many psychologists (and leaders from all disciplines) have long echoed the belief that a teacher needs to walk the path before they can accompany others through similar personal journeys. For myself, I have taken the message of 'removing the log in my eye to see clearly to remove the speck in the eye of others' to be truly helpful advice! It's a process that I continue each and every day.

Emotional literacy has become one of the great additions to personal education in the last few decades. I recall, as a primary school teacher, the delight of pupils as they explored new ideas about feelings through the Personal Social and Health Education (PSHE) lessons. They learned that feelings could be identified, modified, brought under control and interpreted. Contained in this book are a series of exercises that will be familiar to regular users of the Blobs but at a deeper level. They provide both a greater gradation of feelings as well as a way to monitor one's own emotional strengths and vulnerabilities across a day.

Our hope is that by using these visual tools and their questions, over time, each of us will become more understanding of who we are emotionally, and that this might help us to reflect upon an even bigger question – what is the model that we hold within for emotional wholeness and health?

Ian and Pip ☺

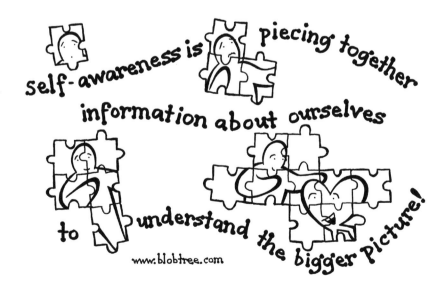

DOI: 10.4324/9781003456551-1

How to Use this Book

Each section of this book has a brief introduction and then a set of questions that accompany each Blob visual tool. Rather than writing over the images, which you may subsequently choose to use with others, it may be helpful to record your thoughts on paper or in a notebook. This also maintains your privacy.

The Blobs are not like mathematical questions, where one answer suffices. As we explore our feelings over a period of time, we may discover that our responses change depending upon the weather, our general moods, the time of the day and many other factors. Feelings are not fixed – they are visitors.

What the combination of questions and Blob visuals hope to reveal is patterns. Each of us has strong emotions which may come to the fore when we are tired, hungry, with certain people, etc. This may take weeks to spot and might even require careful record-making and even asking trustworthy friends to contribute their observations.

Our feelings provide us with information. They signal something to us. Some feelings are pleasurable, others indicate warnings, whilst others are linked to our physical state at that time; for example, many people experience an emotional dip just before eating.

What can we do once we discern these patterns? Noticing is the first stage in our personal growth. Until we correctly see ourselves as we are, the possibility for change and transformation is less likely. If we are unaware of a tendency to become angry around certain people, we can't find ways to modify our responses.

The process of change is fourfold:

1. Trying to identify our unconscious feelings/behaviour,
2. Consciously observing our feelings/behaviour over time,
3. Consciously modifying our behaviour until . . .
4. Our modified behaviour change becomes natural, unconscious.

DOI: 10.4324/9781003456551-2

Self-awareness provides us with an opportunity not only to recognise who we are but also provides us with a base to move from. In order to successfully grow, we take small steps so that the change is incremental, and possible, rather than overwhelming ourselves with targets that we feel unable to sustain.

Pip began the process of noticing his feelings at the age of forty. Over decades, he slowly allowed the change to take place. As he often repeats, "I am in between who I am and who I am becoming". Ian recalls how hearing Pip's phrase, "You are a beautiful human person", at the age of nineteen, kickstarted a change that enabled him to agree by the age of thirty. Both of us continue to allow small changes to become imbedded into our thoughts, feelings, beliefs and lifestyles. This personal evolution, what some call beautification, helps us to love more.

In using this book, take it slow, allow time for reflection, try to accurately spot who you are, ask friends for their outside objective observations rather than compliments, give time to reflect, to pray, to notice and decide where you are aiming. By asking a key question, such as, "What does emotional health look like?" we can find a destination that may prevent us from either burying our feelings or being controlled by them.

The beauty of life is revealed together!

www.blobtree.com

My Charts

My Feelings Diary

This image is based upon thirty-two key feelings. It clearly extends us beyond the four essential emotions of happy, sad, angry and lonely! The purpose of using the diary is to develop our personal awareness of emotions over many years. Having done this in a variety of ways over my life, I have noticed significant changes in who I am and how I feel. Here are a few ways to use this sheet:

A – Photocopy the sheet and annotate it over the week as you notice a feeling. Reflect at the end of the day – which feelings have I had, which are yet to be experienced?

B – Photocopy the sheet and annotate it across a day – which feelings are being expressed within the workplace? You may wish to colour-code it for yourself and for others.

C – Photocopy the sheet and annotate it before and after an event. Use two colours to indicate feelings in the build-up, during an event and following the event. Is this a pattern that happens each time an event occurs?

D – Photocopy the sheet and use a different colour to indicate your feelings when interacting with different people. What signals does your body give you with each person?

The line on the bottom right of the sheet is where one can record the focus for each sheet.

Growth is a mindset that develops

www.blobtree.com

DOI: 10.4324/9781003456551-3

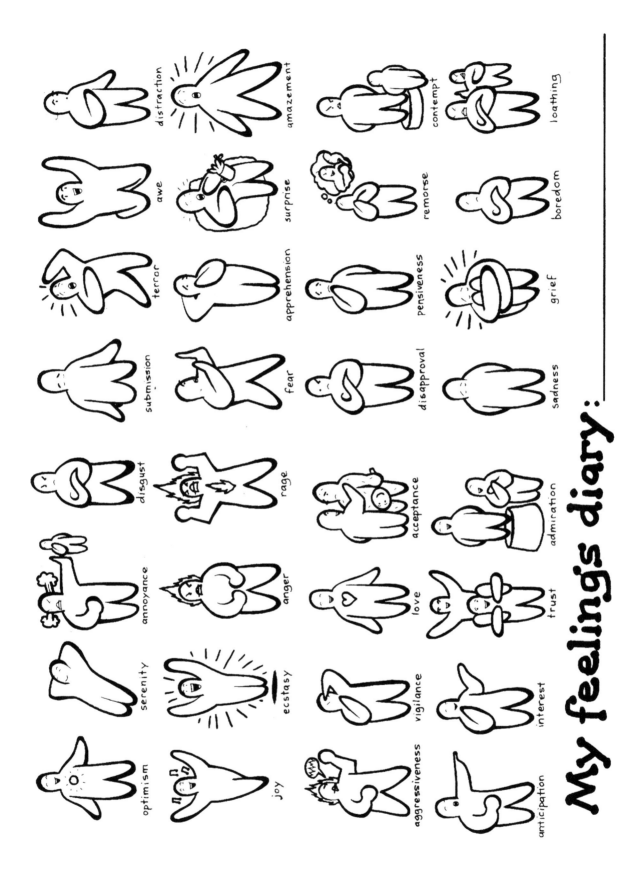

My feelings diary:

Copyright material from Pip Wilson and Ian Long (2024), *My Blob Feelings Workbook*, Routledge

7

My Blob Mood Detector

The Blob Mood Detector is divided into four clear quadrants – moving towards anger, sadness, joy and calm. Use this sheet to identify what moods occur and when they do.

A – Photocopy the Mood Detector sheet. Circle the Blobs in different colours as you identify your feelings over a typical day.

B – Photocopy the sheet. Circle the Blobs that you feel like one hour before meal times. As you reflect upon these later, are these significantly different to the general feelings that you have?

C – Photocopy the sheet. Circle the Blobs in different colours for different people. How does your mood change with each person? Do you respond the same to friends as to colleagues and family?

D – Photocopy the sheet. When do you notice specific feelings occurring across a day/ week? Is there a pattern emerging? What links this feeling?

www.blobtree.com

8

Blob Mood Detector

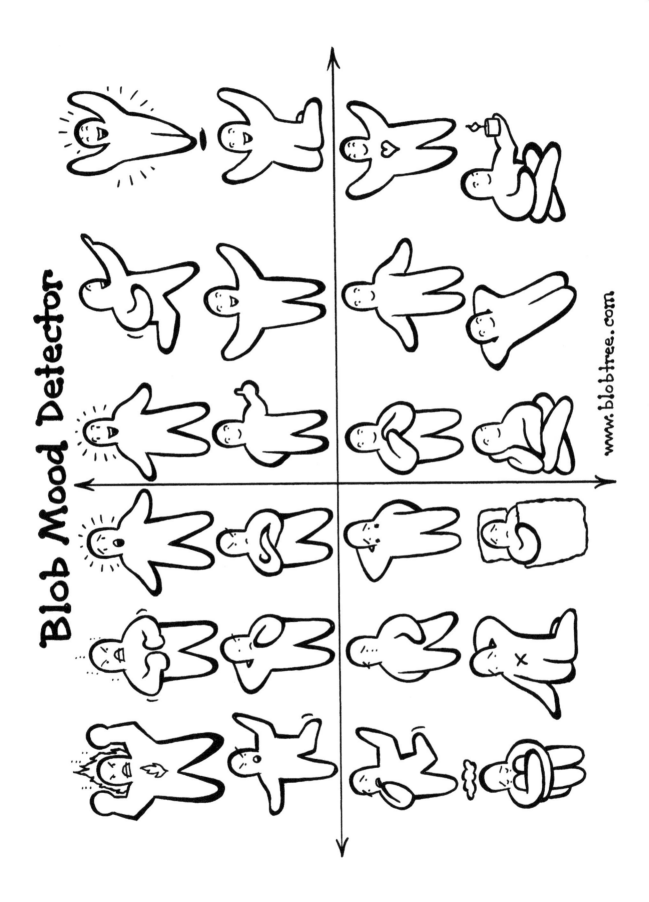

www.blobtree.com

Copyright material from Pip Wilson and Ian Long (2024), *My Blob Feelings Workbook*, Routledge

My Wheel of Emotions

Many people have created concepts based around emotions. This wheel is an illustration with words to extend our literacy. In the centre of the wheel is the strongest form of the emotion. On the outside of the wheel is the weaker form, e.g. rage is a stronger form of anger, whereas annoyance is a weaker form.

Outside the wheel are feelings where some overlap occurs between the feelings on either side, e.g. optimism could be a combination of serenity and interest.

Here are some exercises to explore the wheel:

A – Photocopy the sheet. Choose a rung of the wheel. Colour in the emotions to show the intensity of feelings, e.g. a light shade on the outside and a dark shade on the inside. Gradually build the image up using a different colour for each rung.

B – Photocopy the sheet. Watch a fictional TV programme and colour in an emotion each time it becomes clear during the episode. Which emotions does this story focus upon?

C – Photocopy the sheet. Identify feelings which you do not experience very often. Circle them whenever you come across them in members of your friendship or family circle. Are there any which are missing?

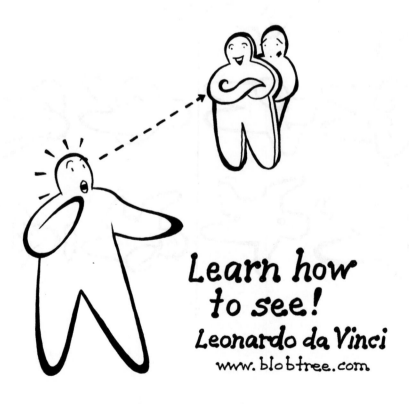

Learn how
to see!
Leonardo da Vinci
www.blobtree.com

Copyright material from Pip Wilson and Ian Long (2024), *My Blob Feelings Workbook*, Routledge

My Anger

This sheet is designed to help identify the level of anger we experience. The word anger means very different things to different people, ranging from 'I'm annoyed' all the way to 'I'm about to become violent'. Using this sheet over a period of time, we can first identify our own levels of anger and then help others to visualise this feeling. Seeing an emotion may help to alert us to the need for change.

Here are some exercises:

A – Photocopy the sheet. Circle the level of anger that you think is your normal experience. Using a different colour, circle the actual emotion on the next number of occasions. Did your thoughts accurately predict the experiences?

B – Photocopy the sheet. Identify someone in your life that you see regularly and who you become angry around. Record the levels of anger that you feel with them. Jot down what it was that caused this intense feeling. Was it their presence, opinions, touch, body language, sarcasm, violence or something else?

C – Photocopy the sheet. Identify a client that you work with / a family member who becomes angry with you. After each incident, circle what level the anger appeared to reach in this individual. Jot down any notes about this experience, especially any words that they used to justify their anger towards you or others.

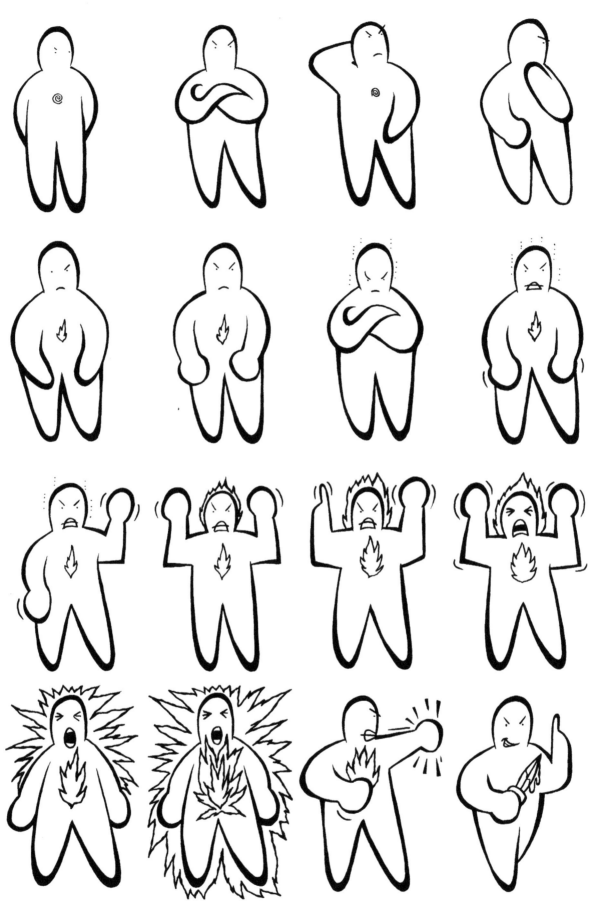

Copyright material from Pip Wilson and Ian Long (2024), *My Blob Feelings Workbook*, Routledge

My Fear

Fear is a very powerful emotion. It occurs in both familiar and unfamiliar settings. Fight, flight or freeze can all be the response to this signal. Some people experience it on a daily basis, whilst for others, it may be a rare feeling. Some sports are advertised using the fear and danger factor. We all encounter it throughout our lives. Here are some exercises to help us reflect upon our personal relationship with fear.

A – Photocopy this sheet. Write a key word next to some of the stages of fear that you can recall, e.g. some people are paralysed with fear at the idea of flying.

B – Photocopy this sheet. During one day, circle the little moments of fear that you experience, whether in a car, at work, at home, with strangers, watching a TV programme, etc. What do you notice about the amount of fear in your day?

C – Photocopy this sheet. During a week, annotate this chart with names of people where you feel a degree of fear. This may be due to their driving, their ideas of pleasure, their threats, etc. Is there anyone that you need to reduce your time with in order to reduce your experience of fear?

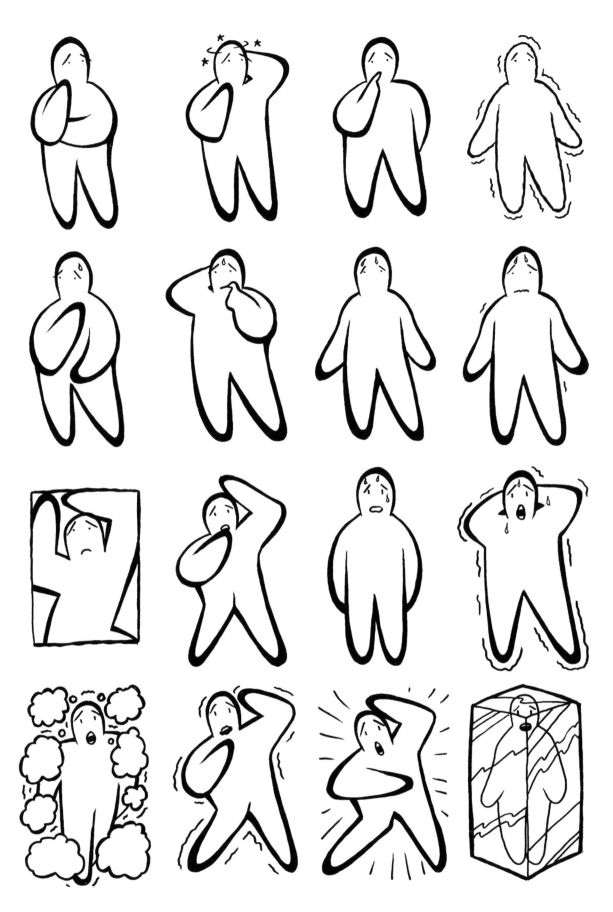

Copyright material from Pip Wilson and Ian Long (2024), *My Blob Feelings Workbook*, Routledge

My Rejection

Rejection is an emotion that can guide our life if we are unaware of it. We can probably all remember the experience of being ignored at school, in a place of work or by a family member. The feeling can be intense, last for long periods of time and lead to a sense of being worthless. We may end up trying to please people in order to maintain a relationship, even when this requires us to do activities that we resent.

Here are some reflective activities for the rejection sheet:

A – Photocopy the sheet. Which rejected Blobs have you felt like in any experiences this week?

B – Photocopy the sheet. Note the Blobs that you feel like in specific places in different colours. Does the feeling of rejection occur only in one place?

C – Photocopy the sheet. Note the feeling of rejection with different people in your work, friendship and home circles. Is there someone who you feel more rejected by than others?

Copyright material from Pip Wilson and Ian Long (2024), *My Blob Feelings Workbook*, Routledge

My Positivity

For some people, optimism is their natural state of being, whereas for most of us, it comes and goes. Being with some people can lift us up just by being in their company. Some people may feel the same way when they spend time with us! Positivity is a quality that we can build into our lives by replacing the content and focus of conversations that we have with others. Just as we value listeners, we can learn to ask more questions and pay attention to what people are telling us.

Here are some activities for reflection:

A – Photocopy the sheet. Circle the Blob that you feel like every hour during one average day. What do you notice about the level of positivity that you've reached?

B – Photocopy the sheet. Circle the Blob that you feel like with different people – friends, family, colleagues. Which group leaves you with the happiest feeling?

C – Photocopy the sheet. Identify a person or experience over the next week for each Blob on this sheet. Did you manage to cover all of them?

D – Photocopy the sheet. Which Blob do you feel like when you are on your own? How does this compare with when you are with others? When are you the happiest?

Copyright material from Pip Wilson and Ian Long (2024), *My Blob Feelings Workbook*, Routledge

My Sadness

Everyone experiences sadness in life. Some years we have our own 'Annus horribilis' when everything seems to go wrong. A large proportion of people live with the sadness of daily depression, requiring some degree of medication. Some people try to run away from sad events and even end friendships when tragedies occur to their friends. Wisdom teaches us to expect things to go wrong, that there will be sadness in life and to press on through it – to persevere. To one degree or another, those who can face sadness and see it as an aspect of existence may open more doors of opportunity than those who retreat from the possibility of suffering.

Here are some reflective activities:

A – Photocopy the sheet. Note down the times when you feel the saddest in a day over a week. Is there a pattern to the time?

B – Photocopy the sheet. Note down the sadness you feel when you are with different people. Do the people who are the most honest and open with you create the saddest response within you, or do those who hide their feelings and experiences from you?

C – Photocopy the sheet. Note the cause of the sadness next to the Blobs that you have felt like over a fortnight. Is there a pattern behind these causes?

www.blobtree.com

Copyright material from Pip Wilson and Ian Long (2024), *My Blob Feelings Workbook*, Routledge

My Basic Blob Feelings Tracker

This sheet helps us to notice and record occasions when we have four basic feelings – happiness, sadness, anger and embarrassment. Emotional literacy requires us first to observe this feeling happening within ourselves. For some people, there may not even be a recognition of any feeling beyond what maintains our personal happiness.

A – Photocopy this sheet. Annotate each emotion when it occurs with a time.
B – Photocopy this sheet. Annotate each emotion when it occurs with a person/group it occurs with.
C – Photocopy this sheet. Annotate each emotion with an intensity rating from 1 (weak) to 5 (strong).
D – Photocopy this sheet. Annotate each emotion with a tally each time it occurs over a week.

Search every where
to locate the problem!

www.blobtree.com

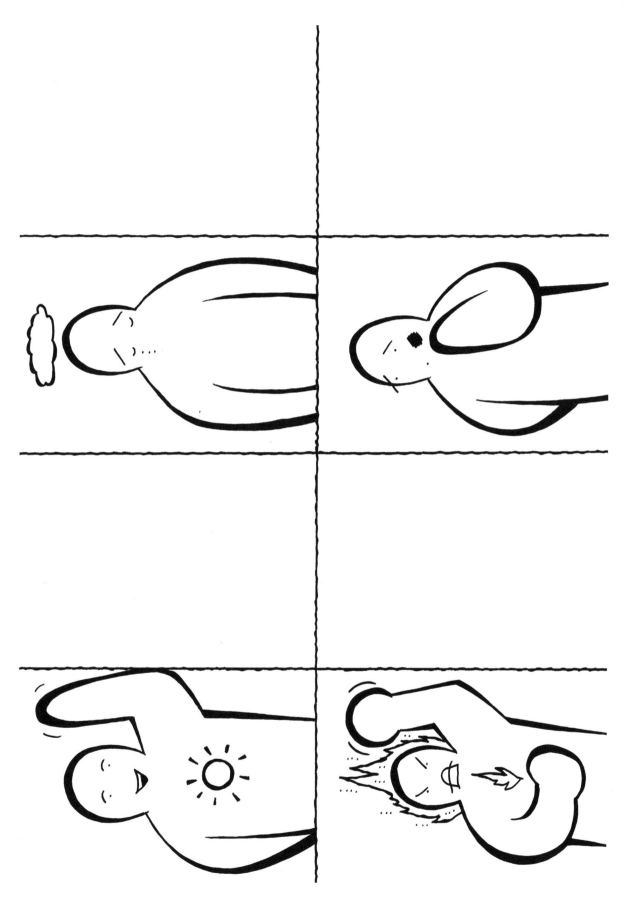

Copyright material from Pip Wilson and Ian Long (2024), *My Blob Feelings Workbook*, Routledge

My Blob Feelings Tracker

This sheet can be used in exactly the same way as the basic one, but recognising that there are eight emotions here rather than four. It is, therefore, advisable to use this after trialling the basic Blob Feelings Tracker. As well as happy, sad, angry and embarrassed, four more have been added – loneliness, shocked, ecstatic and empty. Having already become familiar with four key emotions, it may be helpful to use the same activities to build upon them.

A – Photocopy this sheet. Annotate each emotion when it occurs with a time.

B – Photocopy this sheet. Annotate each emotion when it occurs with a person/group it occurs with.

C – Photocopy this sheet. Annotate each emotion with an intensity rating from 1 (weak) to 5 (strong).

D – Photocopy this sheet. Annotate each emotion with a tally each time it occurs over a week.

For those who wish to extend this beyond the eight feelings, using the 'My Feelings Diary' sheet will further stretch your attention to your feelings.

A powerful thinker can be steered by a tiny emotion

www.blobtree.com

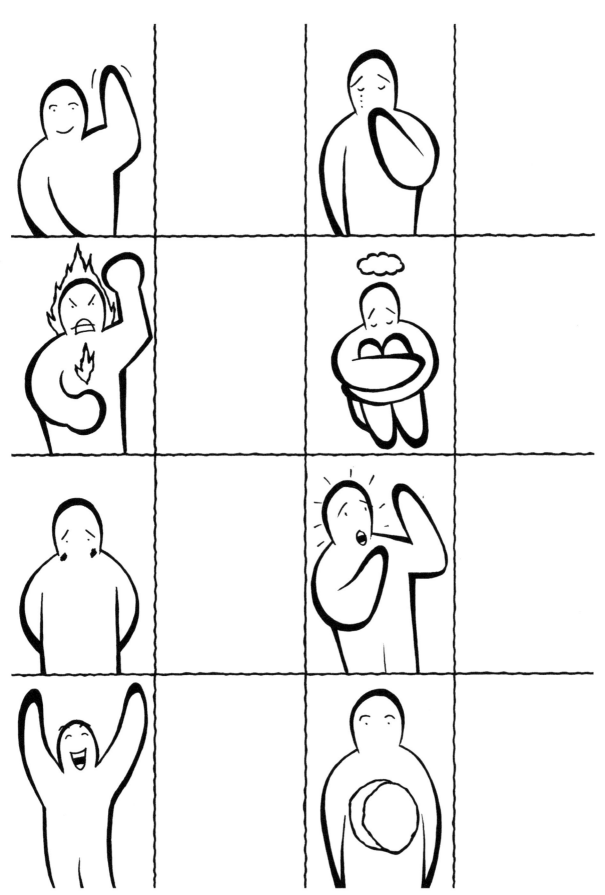

Copyright material from Pip Wilson and Ian Long (2024), *My Blob Feelings Workbook*, Routledge

My Blob Feelings Hierarchy

This sheet should be used after using the Blob Tracking Sheets. Taking the information gleaned from the sheets, photocopy the Blobs representing each feeling, and place them in order of:

A – frequency on the chart
B – strength on the chart.

Reflect upon their balance.

Are you comfortable with the distribution of happiness, sadness, anger, loneliness, ecstasy, embarrassment, emptiness and surprise in your life?

How would you change the distribution? More happiness? Less anger?

Are there ways to change the balance of feelings by making adjustments to our own responses to people, situations and issues within our control?

Make one small change and build that into your life before trying to make huge changes.

My feelings are. signs, guidance,

info clues

www.blobtree.com

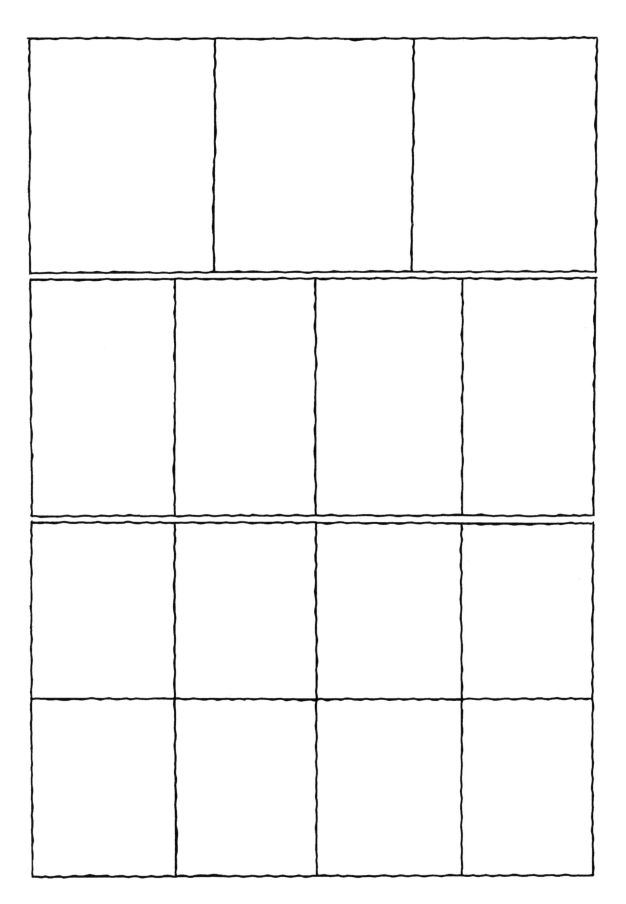

Copyright material from Pip Wilson and Ian Long (2024), *My Blob Feelings Workbook*, Routledge

My Blob Feelings Day

This sheet can be used in the following way to reflect upon the way that the time of day may impact our emotional experiences.

First of all, choose up to four emotions to reflect upon from the Blob Feelings Tracker Sheets. If this is your first attempt, choose only one which occurs frequently most days, e.g. happiness or anger.

Place this in one of the boxes on the left-hand side of the sheet.

As you go through the day, note when the feeling occurs and its strength. There are four quarters to place it according to intensity.

Depending on the day, this may need to be repeated over several days to see if a similar pattern occurs.

Are these emotional changes due to a factor which can be altered? For example, is the emotional exchange due to hunger or tiredness? Could food be introduced at a different time to change this experience?

Once a pattern has been established for an intense emotion, try a second one, etc. Is there a similar pattern for all the feelings?

SUPPORT MATERIAL

2400

1800

1200

0000

Copyright material from Pip Wilson and Ian Long (2024), *My Blob Feelings Workbook*, Routledge

My Blob Trees

Introduction to My Blob Themed Trees

When Pip and I originally designed the Blob Tree in the early 80s, it was as something that could be used with all people, focusing upon feelings. At that time, Pip was working with young people who struggled to express themselves, and so he conceived the idea of a visual solution – an image that could be pointed at to overcome the limitations of language or confidence.

Late one evening, we created the first drawing on a thin piece of card, with spiky branches and clumsily drawn Blobs, searching for appropriate feelings to be depicted. Initially, the Blobs had noses, but then we realised that these were unnecessary to convey body language, so liquid paper edited them out. We were trying to find the simplest way to illustrate feelings and behaviour. Pip trialled this with young people at The Mayflower, a family centre in the East End of London where he worked, and found that it was effective as a tool.

The Blobs were drawn without age, gender, clothes or any limiting features. They could be used globally as the two languages they utilise are feelings and body language, common to us all, the world over. The Tree represents a group, such as a family, a workplace, a class or an organisation. It was the simplest natural structure that we could imagine to house our Blobs.

As time went by, we discovered that by expanding the range of feelings expressed by the Blobs, simple stories began to emerge within the branches. This led us towards the idea of creating scenarios which extended the range of images. Blob Playground and Blob Classroom kicked off a large number of place-specific images. We now have over a thousand images situated in commonly used buildings and environments from around the world.

This section of the book is designed to provide a range of questions to ask yourself on a regular basis about the feelings contained in these Blob Trees. Asking them only once will draw out a snapshot of understanding. Asking them on a regular basis, for example, weekly or monthly, will draw your attention to patterns about your feelings that you may not have noticed. Please choose the Blob Trees that might help you to gain a clearer understanding of who you are emotionally. For example, if anger is a greater concern for you, spend more time exploring these questions rather than an emotion that rarely occurs. In so doing, you will focus your attention productively upon one area which will have a huge effect upon who you are and the relationships that you have. When I changed from being a victim to becoming an adult standing up for myself, the individual who was bullying me had to stop. I didn't change them by force but simply by becoming a person that they could no longer bully.

kindness isn't always valued...

...but don't let that stop you!

www.blobtree.com

DOI: 10.4324/9781003456551-4

General Questions to ask yourself and others about the My Blob Themed Trees

Which Blob:

1: . . . would you like to sit with?

2: . . . do you feel least like?

3: . . . do you feel like at the start of the week?

4: . . . is how you feel when you walk into your home?

5: . . . is how you felt at school?

6: . . . is how you felt yesterday?

7: . . . is how you feel about going on holiday?

8: . . . is how you feel when you wake up in the morning?

9: . . . is how you feel about God?

10: . . . is how you felt when you were bullied?

11: . . . is most like your mother?

12: . . . do you feel like at the end of the week?

13: . . . confuses you?

14: . . . is how you feel with children?

15: . . . is how you feel when you go to bed at night?

16: . . . is how you feel at a place of worship?

17: . . . is how you felt at the age of 5?

18: . . . is how you feel with adults?

19 . . . is how you feel when you are confronted by violence?

20 . . . is how you feel with animals?

21: . . . is when you last felt stupid?

22: . . . is most like your father?

23: . . . is how you felt at the age of 11?

24: . . . is how you feel about being photographed?

25: . . . is how you felt when you were last kissed?

26: . . . is how you feel going shopping?

27: . . . is how you feel when someone tells you off?

28: . . . do you feel like in a pub?

29: . . . is when you have to sort out an argument?

30: . . . is how you felt at the age of 21?

31: . . . is when you get angry?

32: . . . is when you win a competition?

33: . . . is your brother or sister?

34: . . . is when you tell a lie?

35: . . . is when you go to a party?

36: . . . is how you feel when your parents are with you?

37: . . . is when someone points out your mistakes?

38: . . . is when you have free time?

39: . . . is how you feel about dying?

40: . . . is how you feel about going to the hospital?

41: . . . reminds you of Christmas?

42: . . . is how you feel under pressure?

43: . . . is how you feel when you are under pressure to change?

44: . . . is how you feel in a new group of people?

45: . . . is how you feel about getting older?

46: . . . is how you feel being with people who break the law?

47: . . . do you feel like when people ask you to help them?

48: . . . do you feel like today?

49: . . . reminds you of your boss?

50: . . . is how you feel when driving?

51: . . . is how you feel when you see someone with a disability?

Lift
each
other
up

www.blobtree.com

My Blob Tree Anger

The following are suggested questions for reflection. Please use your own as well as examples from the long list on previous pages. The aim is to become aware of our own feelings through reflection.

Photocopy the sheet. You may wish to number the Blobs to speed up your identification.

Which Blobs have you felt like recently?

Which Blobs have you rarely felt like?

Which Blob is how you most commonly feel when angry?

Which Blobs depict the process of anger that you pass through from start to finish?

Which Blob could you imagine shifting to when you feel angry?

We are not alone in how we are feeling
www.blobtree.com

My Blob Tree Fear

The following are suggested questions for reflection. Please use your own as well as examples from the long list on previous pages. The aim is to become aware of our own feelings through reflection.

Photocopy the sheet. You may wish to number the Blobs to speed up your identification.

Which Blobs have you felt like recently?

Which Blobs have you rarely felt like?

Which Blob is how you most commonly feel when fearful?

Which Blobs depict the process of fear that you pass through from start to finish?

Which Blob could you imagine shifting to when you feel fearful?

Copyright material from Pip Wilson and Ian Long (2024), *My Blob Feelings Workbook*, Routledge

My Blob Tree Rejection

The following are suggested questions for reflection. Please use your own as well as examples from the long list on previous pages. The aim is to become aware of our own feelings through reflection.

Photocopy the sheet. You may wish to number the Blobs to speed up your identification.

Which Blobs have you felt like recently?

Which Blobs have you rarely felt like?

Which Blob is how you most commonly feel when rejected?

Which Blobs depict the process of rejection that you pass through from start to finish?

Which Blob could you imagine shifting to when you feel rejected next time?

Sometimes, the best way to deal with my problems,

is to ask for help...

 www.blobtree.com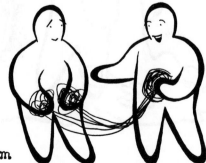

Copyright material from Pip Wilson and Ian Long (2024), *My Blob Feelings Workbook*, Routledge

My Blob Tree Curiosity

The following are suggested questions for reflection. Please use your own as well as examples from the long list on previous pages. The aim is to become aware of our own feelings through reflection.

Photocopy the sheet. You may wish to number the Blobs to speed up your identification.

Which Blobs have you felt like recently?

Which Blobs have you rarely felt like?

Which Blob is how you most commonly feel when curious?

Which Blobs depict the process of curiosity that you pass through from start to finish?

Which Blob could you imagine shifting to when you feel curious next time?

My Blob Tree Positivity

The following are suggested questions for reflection. Please use your own as well as examples from the long list on previous pages. The aim is to become aware of our own feelings through reflection.

Photocopy the sheet. You may wish to number the Blobs to speed up your identification.

Which Blobs have you felt like recently?

Which Blobs have you rarely felt like?

Which Blob is how you most commonly feel when positive?

Which Blobs depict the process of feeling positive that you pass through from start to finish?

Which Blob could you imagine shifting to when you feel positive next time?

Copyright material from Pip Wilson and Ian Long (2024), *My Blob Feelings Workbook*, Routledge

My Blob Tree Sadness

The following are suggested questions for reflection. Please use your own as well as examples from the long list on previous pages. The aim is to become aware of our own feelings through reflection.

Photocopy the sheet. You may wish to number the Blobs to speed up your identification.

Which Blobs have you felt like recently?

Which Blobs have you rarely felt like?

Which Blob is how you most commonly feel when sad?

Which Blobs depict the process of sadness that you pass through from start to finish?

Which Blob could you imagine shifting to when you feel sad next time?

Copyright material from Pip Wilson and Ian Long (2024), *My Blob Feelings Workbook*, Routledge

My Scales

Drawing the Line

The following set of Blob visual tools are scales from high to low (or vice versa). They enable questions to be asked alongside the images. Here is an example of how to use them with the 'Listening' tool. Below are three questions to reflect upon using the method of circling, underlining and ticking a response.

Circle the Blob that shows how well you listen to instructions
Tick the Blob that shows where you would like to aim to be
Underline the Blob that shows how well you listen in group work

Here's how I would suggest that you use this group of visual tools. Look at each scale. Determine what each end of the scale might signify to you. Then read through the questions and answer each one as honestly as you can. After completing them fairly rapidly, come back to them in about a week and review your responses. If they have changed, add a new colour. Often our feelings change due to the ups and downs of life, coupled with our own unique changes.

If you wish to be really daring, ask a good friend to complete them on a separate set of photocopy sheets and see where any huge divergence occurs in your responses. Whilst they are looking in and trying to gauge your feelings from the outside, they may have seen patterns in your behaviour that reveal something that may currently be a blind spot or area of ignorance for you. Rather than object to any of their responses, thank them and allow yourself time to consider them without the pressure of being looked at. Sometimes the views of others might enable you to see clues about who you really are.

This process of letting others rate you for each area needs to be a voluntary act by the individual, not something imposed or mandated by the management team.

For each theme, we have provided three exemplar questions, but please write your own that are appropriate for yourself if none of them seem to apply.

Copyright material from Pip Wilson and Ian Long (2024), My Blob Feelings Workbook, Routledge

DOI: 10.4324/9781003456551-5

Attitude

Circle the Blob that you feel like when you start each day

Underline the Blob that you feel like when you are forced to change your day

Tick the Blob that you feel like during training events

Age

Circle the Blob age when you felt the happiest in life

Underline the Blob age that you wish you could repeat

Tick the Blob age that you struggled in the most

Ability

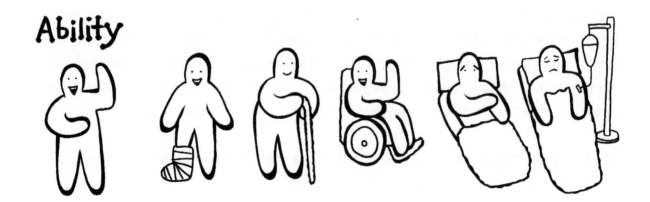

Circle the Blob that depicts how capable you feel at work

Underline the Blob that depicts how capable you feel at home

Tick the Blob that you feel like in unfamiliar situations as a rule

Copyright material from Pip Wilson and Ian Long (2024), *My Blob Feelings Workbook*, Routledge

Behaviour

Circle the Blob that shows the level of bad behaviour you can manage

Underline the Blob that is the behaviour you experience in work/home

Tick the Blob that you would get help with

Broken

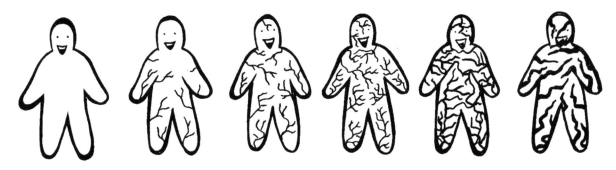

Circle the Blob that depicts how broken you feel emotionally

Underline the Blob that depicts how broken a friend feels

Tick the Blob that you feel like in the morning when you wake up

Bullying

Circle the Blob that you experienced at school as a child

Underline the Blob that shows the worst bullying you've known as an adult

Tick the Blob that shows how you currently feel

Copyright material from Pip Wilson and Ian Long (2024), *My Blob Feelings Workbook*, Routledge

Bystander

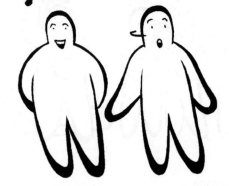

Circle the Blob that depicts how you react when you notice bullying

Underline the Blob that shows a helpful reaction

Tick the Blob that you feel is the best response around violence

Caring

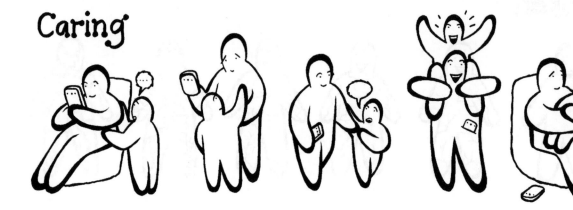

Circle the Blob that you see often around you

Underline the Blob that depicts the best standard of care in your opinion

Tick the Blob that you behave like around close friends/family

Charitable

Circle the Blob that reminds you of a colleague/friend who is charitable

Underline the Blob that you feel like at the end of a day

Tick the Blob that you feel like when asked to help out for a long project

Copyright material from Pip Wilson and Ian Long (2024), *My Blob Feelings Workbook*, Routledge

Compassion

Circle the Blob compassion that shows how you recently helped a friend

Underline the Blob that shows the most compassion that you have received

Tick the Blob compassion that you offer to strangers in need

Draw the Line: closed to open

www.blobtree.com

Circle the Blob that depicts how open you feel about hearing new ideas

Underline the Blob that depicts how open you are to small changes

Tick the Blob that you feel like about faith

Dance

Circle the Blob that depicts how free you feel about dancing in public

Underline the Blob that depicts how free you feel about dancing at home

Tick the Blob that you would like to feel like when dancing

Copyright material from Pip Wilson and Ian Long (2024), *My Blob Feelings Workbook*, Routledge

Depression

Circle the Blob that depicts how you have felt at your worst moment

Underline the Blob that depicts how you function on most days

Tick the Blob that you feel others want you to be like

Emptiness

Circle the Blob that depicts how empty you feel where you work

Underline the Blob that depicts how empty you feel at home

Tick the Blob that you feel how empty friends feel like

Fear

Circle the Blob that depicts how fearful you feel out walking in the day

Underline the Blob that depicts how fearful you feel at home

Tick the Blob that depicts how fearful you feel out walking at night

Copyright material from Pip Wilson and Ian Long (2024), *My Blob Feelings Workbook*, Routledge

Fitness

Circle the Blob that depicts how fit you feel overall

Underline the Blob that depicts how fit you would like to feel

Tick the Blob that shows how fit you reasonably could be like

Fulfilment

Circle the Blob that you've felt like at your most fulfilled

Underline the Blob that depicts how fulfilled you currently feel

Tick the Blob that you can foresee yourself becoming in the near future

Generous

Circle the Blob that depicts how you like to share your money

Underline the Blob that depicts how you have recently helped a stranger

Tick the Blob that you have experienced from others

Copyright material from Pip Wilson and Ian Long (2024), *My Blob Feelings Workbook*, Routledge

Grit

Circle the Blob that depicts how you persevere against difficulties

Underline the Blob that shows how your friends persevere against difficulties

Tick the Blob that depicts how you persevere against long-term issues

Helpful

Circle the Blob that depicts how helpful a friend/colleague is

Underline the Blob that depicts how helpful you try to be

Tick the Blob that reminds you of an unhelpful person known to you

Blob Impostor www.blobtree.com

Circle the Blob that depicts a situation you have felt inexperienced in

Underline the Blob that depicts how a current boss/teacher seems to be

Tick the Blob that you feel like most days

Copyright material from Pip Wilson and Ian Long (2024), *My Blob Feelings Workbook*, Routledge

Kindness

Circle the Blob that depicts your natural level of kindness

Underline the Blob that depicts how kind you feel at home

Tick the Blob that you feel like when asked to be kind when tired

Mental health

Circle the Blob that depicts your general state of mental health

Underline the Blob that depicts how you've felt at your best recently

Tick the Blob that you feel is a reasonable level to function at

Mind v Heart

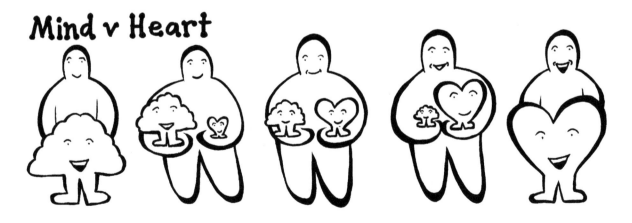

Circle the Blob that depicts how you tend to respond to fun ideas

Underline the Blob that depicts how you respond to conflict

Tick the Blob that you feel like when making important decisions

Copyright material from Pip Wilson and Ian Long (2024), *My Blob Feelings Workbook*, Routledge

Mindfulness

Circle the Blob that depicts how much background noise you work in

Underline the Blob that depicts your quietest period each day

Tick the Blob that you choose when you have free time

Noise

Circle the Blob that depicts your favourite level of noise at home

Underline the Blob that depicts the level of noise to help you focus

Tick the Blob that is the noise level that you find most challenging

Observing

Circle the Blob that depicts an appropriate reflecting level each day

Underline the Blob that depicts your general level of reflection

Tick the Blob that you have been before today's reflecting

Copyright material from Pip Wilson and Ian Long (2024), *My Blob Feelings Workbook*, Routledge

Openness

Circle the Blob that depicts how open to new friends you are

Underline the Blob that depicts how open to being told what to do you are

Tick the Blob that shows how open you are to cultural change

Personal space

Circle the Blob that depicts your personal space at work/school

Underline the Blob that depicts your personal space at home

Tick the Blob that depicts your favourite personal space

Positivity

Circle the Blob that depicts how positive you feel right now

Underline the Blob that depicts how positive you generally feel

Tick the Blob that depicts how positive you feel about Mondays

Copyright material from Pip Wilson and Ian Long (2024), *My Blob Feelings Workbook*, Routledge

Prayerful

Circle the Blob that depicts your response to prayer

Underline the Blob that depicts how you've prayed today

Tick the Blob that shows the level of prayer you use in a crisis

Reflecting

Circle the Blob that depicts how you reflect best

Underline the Blob that depicts how you have reflected today

Tick the Blob that shows your least reflective approach

Rejection

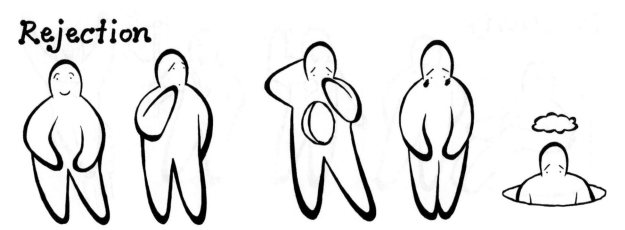

Circle the Blob that depicts how you felt about being rejected recently

Underline the Blob that depicts how you felt after reflecting on being rejected

Tick the Blob that you would like to feel like if someone rejects you

Copyright material from Pip Wilson and Ian Long (2024), *My Blob Feelings Workbook*, Routledge

Relationships

Circle the Blob that depicts your favourite relationship

Underline the Blob that depicts how you spend most of your free time

Tick the Blob dynamic that drains you of most of your energy

Resilience

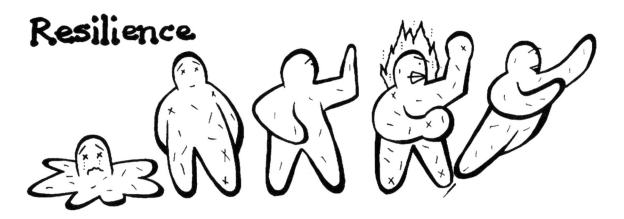

Circle the Blob that depicts how you fight back against an attack

Underline the Blob that depicts how you wish you responded against a threat

Tick the Blob that you feel like being threatened on a regular basis

Responsibility

Circle the Blob that depicts how you respond to a need at work

Underline the Blob that depicts how you respond to a need at home

Tick the Blob that shows how you respond to your own needs

Copyright material from Pip Wilson and Ian Long (2024), *My Blob Feelings Workbook*, Routledge

Sadness

Circle the Blob that depicts how sad you currently feel

Underline the Blob that shows how sad you feel generally

Tick the Blob that depicts how you feel after watching the news

Scars

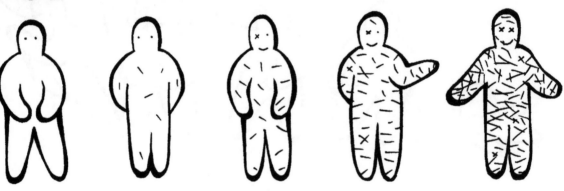

Circle the Blob that depicts how wounded you feel inside

Underline the Blob that depicts how wounded you feel by just one person

Tick the Blob that shows how you feel others perceive your scars

Self acceptance

Circle the Blob that depicts how you accept yourself, warts and all

Underline the Blob that depicts how you would like to feel about yourself

Tick the Blob that shows how you felt about yourself as a child

Copyright material from Pip Wilson and Ian Long (2024), *My Blob Feelings Workbook*, Routledge

Self Harm

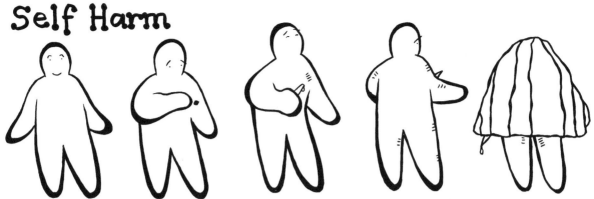

Circle the Blob that depicts someone you know
Underline the Blob that depicts a level you've tried
Tick the Blob that shows the level that you think needs help

Self-regulation

Circle the Blob that depicts how you've been self-regulating
Underline the Blob that depicts how others perceive you
Tick the Blob that shows what level it feels like on a bad day

Sensing

Circle the Blob that depicts which of your senses you use the most
Underline the Blob that depicts your least used sense
Tick the Blob that shows your favourite sense

Copyright material from Pip Wilson and Ian Long (2024), My Blob Feelings Workbook, Routledge

Shame

Circle the Blob that depicts your strongest feeling of shame

Underline the Blob that depicts how you felt as a child

Tick the Blob that shows how you could imagine feeling in the future

Self-awareness scale www.blobtree.com

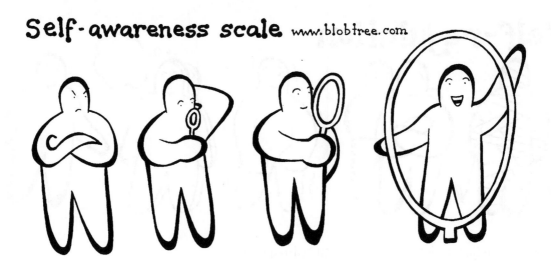

Circle the Blob that shows how well you know yourself

Underline the Blob that depicts how well you wish to know all about yourself

Tick the Blob that shows how well you know your strengths

Social Relationships

Circle the Blob that depicts how you relate to people at work

Underline the Blob that depicts how you relate at home

Tick the Blob that shows your preferred approach in relationships

Copyright material from Pip Wilson and Ian Long (2024), *My Blob Feelings Workbook*, Routledge

Stillness

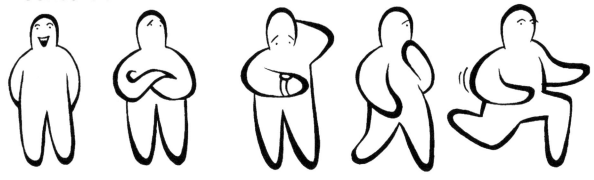

Circle the Blob that depicts how still your day tends to be

Underline the Blob that depicts your stillest point today

Tick the Blob that shows your comfortable zone

Violence

Circle the Blob that depicts the type of violence that scares you

Underline the Blob that depicts a recent experience of violence

Tick the Blob that shows a level that you've used recently

Copyright material from Pip Wilson and Ian Long (2024), *My Blob Feelings Workbook*, Routledge

My Cycles

My Blob Daily Cycle

Photocopy the sheet.

Look at this simple cycle for a day.

Circle the elements which often occur in your daily cycle.

Tick the elements that you enjoy.

Underline aspects that you would like to vary or change in the future.

Annotate anything important to you that is missing.

DOI: 10.4324/9781003456551-6

SUPPORT MATERIAL

Copyright material from Pip Wilson and Ian Long (2024), *My Blob Feelings Workbook*, Routledge

My Blob Anxiety Cycle

Photocopy the sheet.

Look at this simple anxiety cycle.

Circle the elements which occur for you during anxiety attacks/anxious moments.

Tick the elements that you dislike the most.

Underline one aspect that you would like to change/reduce in the future.

Annotate anything important to you that is missing.

Review in a month to see if anything has changed or is clearer upon further reflection.

SUPPORT MATERIAL

The Anxiety Cycle
www.blobtree.com

Copyright material from Pip Wilson and Ian Long (2024), *My Blob Feelings Workbook*, Routledge

My Blob Breaking the Anxiety Cycle

Photocopy the sheet

Look at this simple breaking the anxiety cycle to identify key changes that could be made.

Circle the strategies that you use to help you calm down.

Tick one new approach that you could use (reflecting upon the trigger, reducing the compulsion to run away, learning to calm yourself down, prayer and mindfulness, having a talk partner to coach you to calm, writing your thoughts down, observing patterns in your behaviour, etc.).

Underline one approach that you think won't work for you at the moment.

Annotate anything important to you that is missing that helps to calm you down.

Review in a month to see if anything has changed or is clearer upon further reflection.

Copyright material from Pip Wilson and Ian Long (2024), *My Blob Feelings Workbook*, Routledge

My Blob Anger Cycle

Photocopy the sheet.

Look at this simple cycle of anger.

Circle the elements which occur for you during anger outbursts.

Tick the elements that you struggle with the most.

Underline one aspect that you would like to change/reduce in the future.

Annotate anything important to you that is missing that you have noticed.

Review in a month to see if anything has changed or is clearer upon further reflection. Add your observations to this image.

Copyright material from Pip Wilson and Ian Long (2024), *My Blob Feelings Workbook*, Routledge

My Blob Cycle of Depression

Photocopy the sheet

Look at this simple cycle of Depression.

Circle the elements which occur for you during depression cycles.

Tick the elements that you struggle with the most.

Underline one point where you have noticed the cycle changing for the better. Identify what occurred to make that difference.

Annotate anything important to you that is missing.

Review in a month to see if anything has changed or is clearer upon further reflection and add to this diagram.

SUPPORT MATERIAL

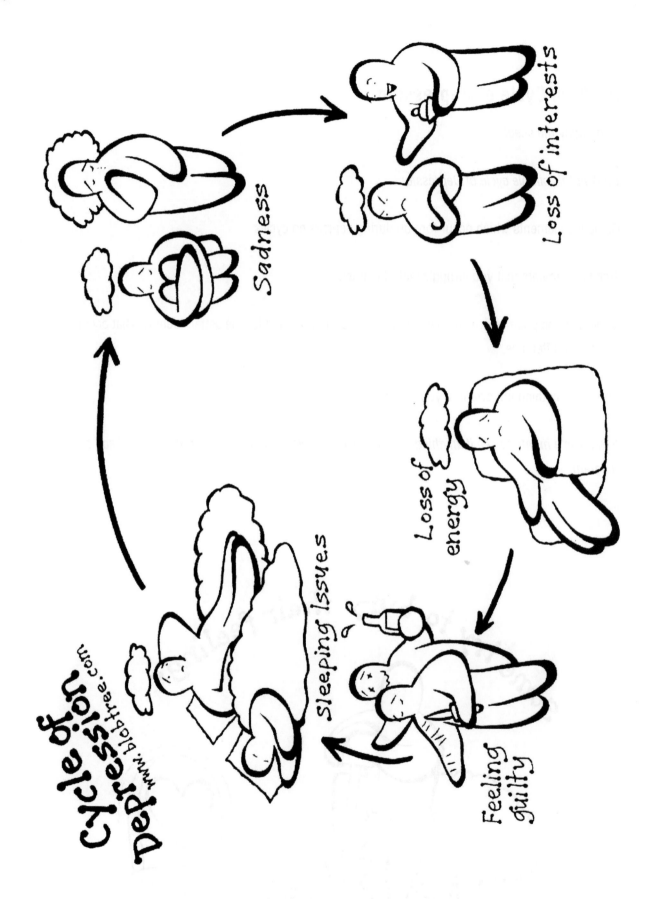

Copyright material from Pip Wilson and Ian Long (2024), *My Blob Feelings Workbook*, Routledge

My Blob Cycle of Disappointment

Photocopy the sheet

Look at this disappointment cycle.

Circle the elements which occur for you following a disappointment.

Tick the elements that upset you the most.

Underline one point in the cycle where you have changed something to move you out of the cycle and found that it worked.

Annotate anything important to you that is missing.

Review in a month to see if anything has changed or is clearer upon further reflection.

Copyright material from Pip Wilson and Ian Long (2024), *My Blob Feelings Workbook*, Routledge

My Scenarios

How to Use this Section

There is no one way to use these sheets. Here are three approaches to start you off with each of the backgrounds. There are a myriad more ways to use these visual toolkits.

Basic approach

This is the basic approach. Start with the Blob Tree Background, as it should be familiar to you. Decide what your question for reflection will be. For example, you might ask, 'How did I feel yesterday?' Provide a range of Blobs from the available sets for yourself to choose one or more Blobs from. Then stick them onto the Tree one by one, allowing time for personal reflection.

DOI: 10.4324/9781003456551-7

Story approach

Using the same start, ask a question where you have to choose several Blobs, e.g. "Choose several Blobs to show how your feelings changed throughout school/work today." Provide a range of Blobs from the individual sets for yourself to select from. Create the emotional story of your day.

Where on the Tree approach

Use the same start, and provide a question as well as the sheets of Blobs. When it comes to placing the Blob onto the Tree, think about where on the Tree you think that Blob feeling might go and why. This might be difficult for the first Blob you place but increasingly easy as the rest may orientate themselves around this first choice.

You may appreciate seeing the Blobs laid around the Background, but be aware that too many Blobs can be confusing.

Each sheet has a different emphasis. **The Blob Tree** is about general feelings. **The Blob Bridge** is focused upon moments of change and transition – going from one side to the next. **The Blob Pitch** is an opportunity to reflect upon one's beliefs – 'Where am I on the pitch of faith?' **The Blob Playground** is useful to ask yourself about your childhood and school life. **The Blob Home** can be useful to reflect upon our life and feelings at home. A basic set of questions has been provided with each sheet except The Blob Tree.

Copyright material from Pip Wilson and Ian Long (2024), *My Blob Feelings Workbook*, Routledge

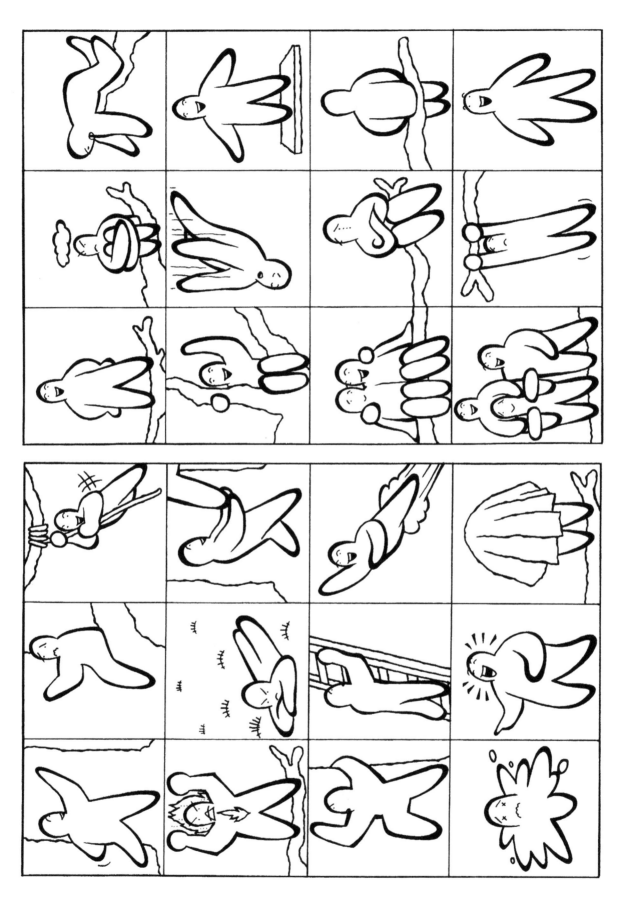

Copyright material from Pip Wilson and Ian Long (2024), *My Blob Feelings Workbook*, Routledge

My Blob Bridge

Photocopy the sheet.

Use the figures from either My Blob Tree or My Feelings Diary.

The Blob Bridge represents a crossing from one side to the other – a change or transition. Using a current or historic example of change, reflect on how you feel/felt about it.

You may like to use these questions in order to select your Blobs:

Which Blob did you feel like when you heard the news about the change?

Which Blob did you feel like after the process of change began?

Which Blob do you feel like now that it has been finished?

If you could choose one Blob to be now, which one would it be?

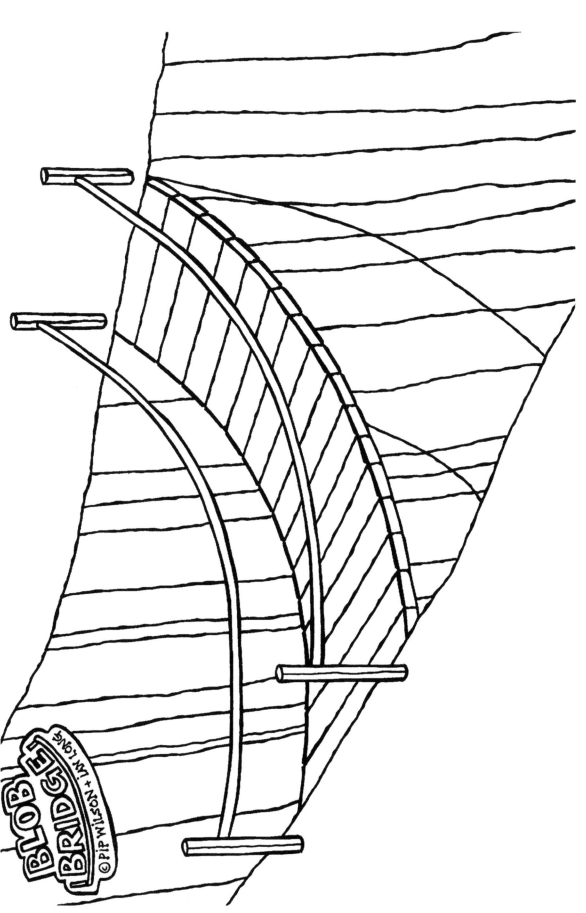

Copyright material from Pip Wilson and Ian Long (2024), *My Blob Feelings Workbook*, Routledge

My Blob Pitch

Photocopy the sheet.

Use the figures on the next page.

The Blob Pitch represents all of our beliefs. The image is broken up into four sections – the stands where people are watching but not participating; the changing rooms where people are getting ready to come on; the pitch where people are participating in a variety of ways; and the showers where people are cooling off having recently participated on the pitch.

You may like to use these questions in order to select your Blobs:

Where would you currently place yourself on the Blob Pitch of belief?

Which Blob do you feel like most of the time?

Which Blob did you use to be?

If you could choose one Blob to be now, which one would it be?

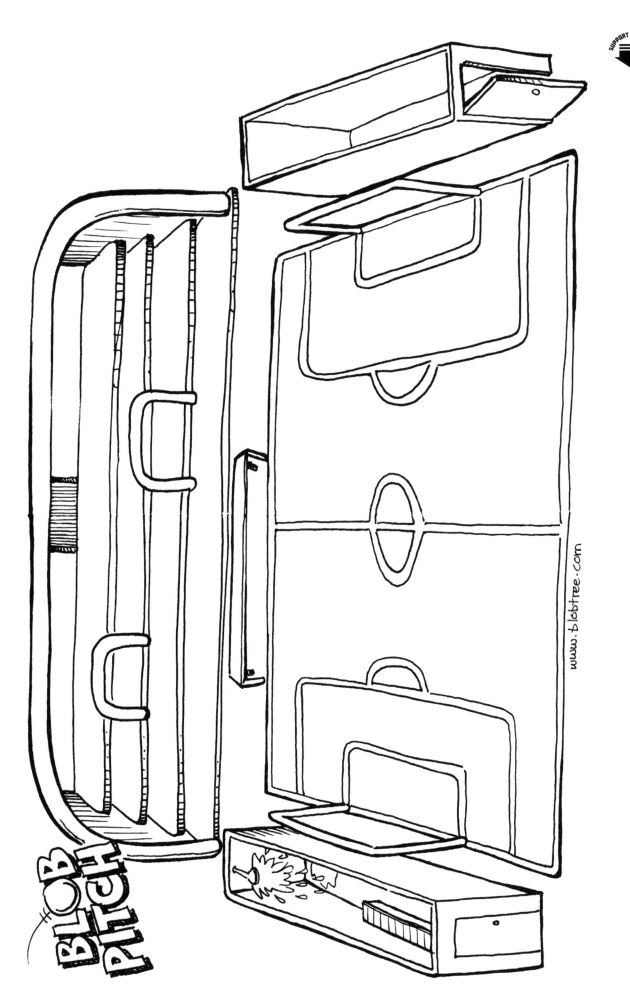

Copyright material from Pip Wilson and Ian Long (2024), *My Blob Feelings Workbook*, Routledge

SUPPORT MATERIAL

Copyright material from Pip Wilson and Ian Long (2024), *My Blob Feelings Workbook*, Routledge

My Blob Playground

Photocopy the sheet.

Use the figures by photocopying them from either My Blob Tree or My Feelings Diary.

The Blob Playground represents how we felt about our childhood. The playground was where we made friends, played games and spent many hours of our lives.

You may like to use these questions in order to select your Blobs:

Which Blob did you feel like when you were at school

Which Blob did you feel like when you went to secondary school?

Which Blob did you feel like when you left school?

If you could choose one Blob to be playing with, which one would it be?

Copyright material from Pip Wilson and Ian Long (2024), *My Blob Feelings Workbook*, Routledge

SUPPORT MATERIAL

BLOB PLAYGROUND

© Pip Wilson + Ian Long

www.blobtree.com

Copyright material from Pip Wilson and Ian Long (2024), *My Blob Feelings Workbook*, Routledge

My Blob Home

Photocopy the sheet.

Use the figures from either My Blob Tree or My Feelings Diary.

The Blob Home is perhaps the most personal of places for reflection and is probably best left until being familiar with at least The My Blob Tree sheet. For most people, the home is the most precious place to be, but for some of us, it can be a place of fear and pain.

You may like to use these questions in order to select your Blobs:

Where is your happiest place to be in your home?

Which Blob did you feel like as a child in your home?

Which Blob do you feel like now in your home?

Which Blob have you lived with in your home that you didn't find easy?

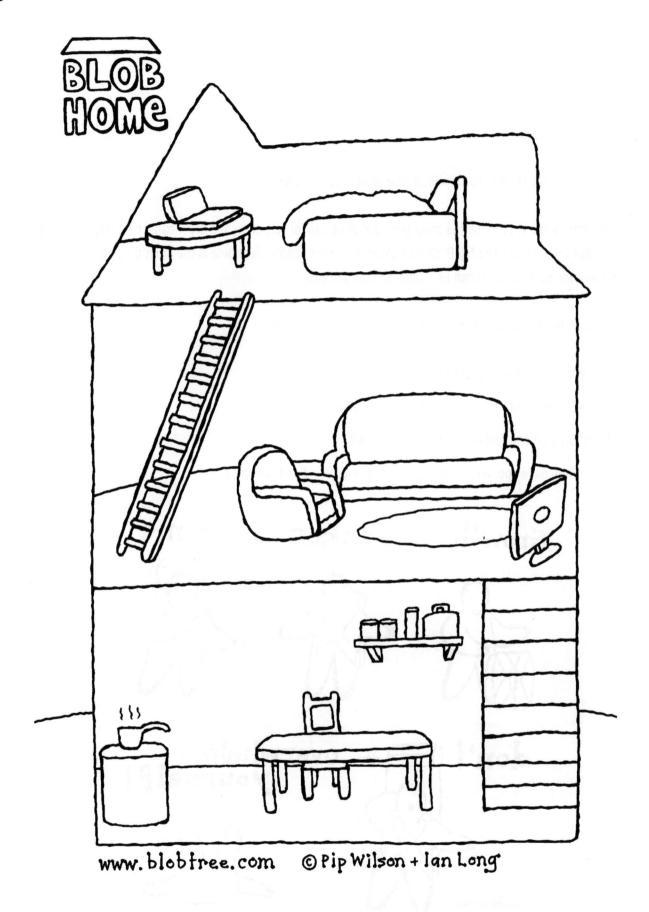

www.blobtree.com   © Pip Wilson + Ian Long

Copyright material from Pip Wilson and Ian Long (2024), *My Blob Feelings Workbook*, Routledge

My Theory

My Blob Theory

Theories of life are common. Some people use them to help improve their self-awareness. Theories are often a way of explaining patterns in human behaviour. The more we understand them, the more we can apply them to our own life and benefit from their insights.

It takes a long time for new theories to be absorbed naturally through a society. Some ideas are being developed now that might take decades to get beyond the realm of academia. All of these theories have been around for several decades and, to a greater or lesser extent, have helped professionals in their work.

In this section, some familiar and unfamiliar ideas have been turned into Blob visual tools for reflection. Each one provides a degree of insight. Some questions have been provided with each visual tool to help the process of reflection.

Blob Maslow looks at the hierarchy of needs. The Blob Attitude chart helps to identify where our energy levels and attitude overlap. The Blob Heart helps us to consider who we let into our heart. Blob Level 5 looks at our conversation and communication. The Blob How Close Diagram aids reflection upon our intimate friendships. My Ideal Holiday examines an area that few consider, even though trips are often the highlight of the year. My Blob SWOT is a tool to analyse many areas of life through positives and negatives. Blob Life is a way to consider the whole of our life at whatever stage we are at.

DOI: 10.4324/9781003456551-8

My Blob Maslow

Photocopy the sheet

Abraham Maslow devised this way of thinking about the "Hierarchy of Our Needs" in 1943, during World War Two, when priorities shifted from the cultural breadth of peacetime to surviving a war. The hierarchy diagram is split between needs which are essential for survival and the needs of growth. As we look at the diagram, we will perceive it through either survival or growth, depending upon where we are in our personal and national history.

Using the sheet for reflection. Here are some thought starters; please add your own:

Look at the sheet and mark on it the different stages of your life and how these correspond in some way to the five levels. For example, when I was born, I depended entirely upon my family for survival.

Which level did you spend much of your day at? For example, on a Sunday, I join lots of friends worshipping God in my local church, which I see both as belonging and becoming whole.

Which level would you find it hardest to lose? For example, having the sense of security enables me to confidently explore growth areas.

Which level would you describe how you will spend this evening? For example, I'm inviting friends around – the belonging level.

SUPPORT MATERIAL

Copyright material from Pip Wilson and Ian Long (2024), *My Blob Feelings Workbook*, Routledge

My Blob Attitude

Photocopy the sheet.

The following image is worth exploring to see where our attitudes come from at any specific moment. What is interesting to note is that some people tend to fall on the same square every time they reflect, whereas others keep on changing. Becoming aware of who we are in our energy levels and attitude may be difficult at first, but with help from someone who knows us well, we may begin to see ourselves more clearly.

Look at the image, taking time to see the energy levels and attitudes that combine to create the grid.

Which Blob do you feel like today?

Which Blob do you often feel like in the morning? Evening?

Which Blob would you like to be? Is there a way to move towards that goal?

Revisit this sheet over time to see if your self-assessment has changed

Copyright material from Pip Wilson and Ian Long (2024), *My Blob Feelings Workbook*, Routledge

My Blob Heart

Photocopy the sheet.

Look at the sheet and identify the feelings and behaviours of each of the Blobs. You may wish to annotate the diagram with your thoughts.

Can you put a name to each Blob if they symbolise people who are in a variety of relationships with you; for example, family, friends and colleagues?

Can you put a name to each Blob to describe situations where you feel able to share your heart at different depths? For example, the Blobs in the bottom right-hand corner might represent a good friend who you play sport with and only banter in conversation.

Can you identify each Blob in terms of self-awareness? For example, I got stuck in trying to understand why I felt difficulty in celebrating my own birthday. Or, I would like to be friends with myself.

SUPPORT MATERIAL

Blob Heart
www.blobtree.com

Copyright material from Pip Wilson and Ian Long (2024), *My Blob Feelings Workbook*, Routledge

My Level 5

Pip's Level 5 diagram explores the content of our own conversation with a simple structure.

Level 1: Cliché – this is the start of most conversations with someone new. We may ask about the weather, use the word fine a lot, use the word hey, okay or the latest trending phrase. In self-conversation, we may use expressions that motivate us, such as, 'come on, you can do this' or 'we're good'.

Level 2: Facts – many conversations are centred around facts. We may ask for directions, tell people information about ourselves, ask people to buy products for us at the shops, etc. In self-conversation, we may develop an interest in a hobby which we record in a written or digital form. We may study a subject so that we can, first of all, convince ourselves before then sharing it with others.

Level 3: Opinions – we have opinions on many subjects which will range from topics which are well-researched to immediate reactions to a variety of issues. Opinions can become the starting point of a conflict. In self-conversation, we may have opinions about ourselves which we have picked up from others that may include incorrect negative views, wrong assumptions and criticisms that we have taken onboard and speak to ourselves, reinforcing opinions which may have been provided to us decades before.

Level 4: Feelings – personal feelings are generally expressed to a few people who we trust. When we share our inner selves, our conversations usually begin with the word, 'I'. In self-conversation, we may speak in affirming or unaffirming ways, such as, 'Why do I always do that?' or 'I am so stupid' or 'I am a beautiful human person', depending upon how we feel about ourselves.

Level 5: Complete Openness – it is rare to be able to share openly with a friend about anything and everything. Some people have a best friend going all the way back to their childhood. Pip created a group called 'Level 5' for this express purpose. It was something that he believed was important to provide. In self-conversation, we may speak completely openly with ourselves, as there is no one but ourselves to hear, or we may try to hide information, justify our actions, have blind spots which we need others to identify in us, etc.

Using these ideas, listen to yourself over many weeks and annotate the diagram with phrases that you use with yourself. Gradually form a picture of how you converse with yourself, not only when you are doing the shopping but in the occasional thoughts when you doubt yourself, defend yourself internally, become angry with or praise yourself.

SUPPORT MATERIAL

Copyright material from Pip Wilson and Ian Long (2024), *My Blob Feelings Workbook*, Routledge

My How Close

This is a very simple tool but one that can help to reveal aspects of relationships that we might not have consciously noticed.

Photocopy the sheet.

Going one by one, think of a family member, friend or colleague and place them on the diagram using the following different criteria:

How much do you share your thoughts and feelings with them and vice versa?

How much do you enjoy their company and laugh together?

How much do you respect their opinions?

For each criterion, you may find that each individual changes position on the diagram.

www.blobtree.com

BLOB HOW CLOSE?
www.blobtree.com © IAN LONG + © PIP WILSON

Copyright material from Pip Wilson and Ian Long (2024), *My Blob Feelings Workbook*, Routledge

My Ideal Holiday

There are many areas of life that happen on a regular basis, but we often copy someone else's idea of the experience rather than reflect upon what we are looking for ourselves. Holidays are one of these things. Almost everyone looks forward to a break, but afterwards, many feel that they either feel more tired from the experience or they didn't get what they were imagining. This sheet provides a few key reflections on what type of holiday we really enjoy.

Photocopy the sheet.

Tick the images that we find pleasurable; for example, I enjoy visiting cities. Add in your own words if there is no relevant image.

Cross the images that we definitely don't enjoy; for example, I live in the countryside, so I want a change from that.

Now, take the images that you find pleasurable and rank them from your favourite element to the least element. You might want to cut out the squares to help you to do this.

If you like to go on holiday with a spouse, partner or friend, it will be a good idea to get them to try the same set of questions and then see where you overlap, but only after you know your own mind on the matter.

A compromise may work better for both of you if one of you prefers the countryside to the city. Either do half in one place and half in another, create two long weekends or take turns in deciding where to go for a holiday.

Quick to Pause   Slow Reflection

www.blobtree.com

Copyright material from Pip Wilson and Ian Long (2024), *My Blob Feelings Workbook*, Routledge

My SWOT

A SWOT diagram looks at a change through the eyes of Strengths, Weaknesses, Opportunities and Threats.

Photocopy the sheet.

Write the particular change that you are facing at the top of the sheet.

Work through the four quadrants, reflecting upon the positives and negatives of the change. Try to find strong points for both sides, even if you remain adamantly against the change. It develops our thinking to perceive positives on both sides of the coin, and this may make us better judges when it comes to finalising our opinions.

If you can't think of anything in one or more of the quadrants, it might help to get other people's ideas on this matter.

SUPPORT MATERIAL

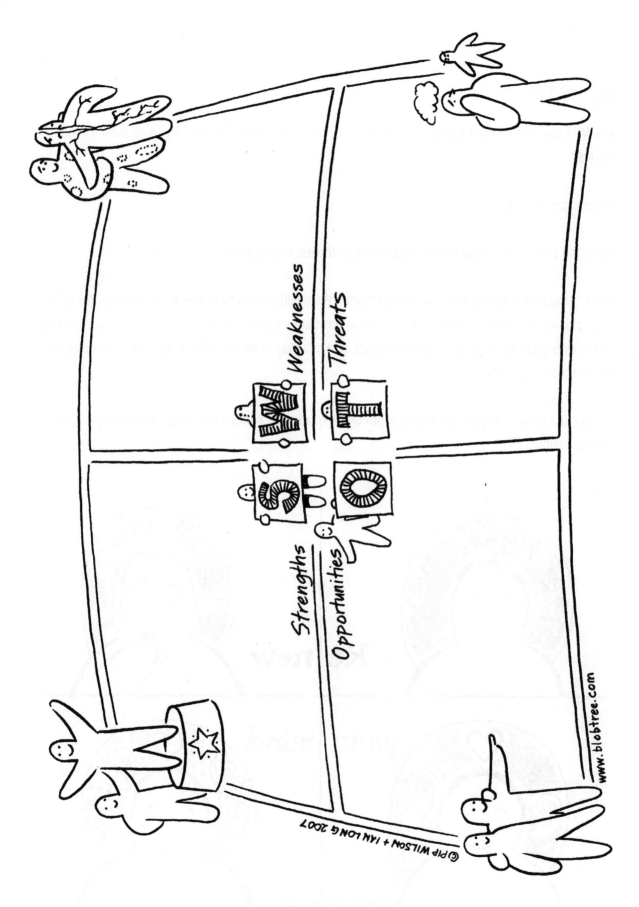

Copyright material from Pip Wilson and Ian Long (2024), *My Blob Feelings Workbook*, Routledge

My Blob Life

This visual tool enables you to look at life in a one-image experience. You will give each Blob and the stage that they are at the interpretation that you desire.

Photocopy the sheet.

Look at the sheet to register the different phases of life and death that the Blobs are passing through.

Determine where you are on the journey of life.

Annotate what you see as your favourite phase of life.

Annotate the phase of life you have struggled in most so far.

Annotate a phase yet to come that you are looking forward to.

Copyright material from Pip Wilson and Ian Long (2024), *My Blob Feelings Workbook*, Routledge

My Blob Cards

My Blob Cards

The following pages contain the key thirty-two emotions which can be photocopied and cut up as cards to use in the following exercises. Some of the activities are for pairs, some for small groups and some for a large group. All of them can be adapted for personal use. For example, the first task could be carried out solo by using a table. Write opposite emotion words on two pieces of paper, place them at either end of the table, then select one card at a time and place them between those two extremes which best fit the card.

1 Emotional literacy exercise for a large group – give out an emotion card to each person or pair. Then, one pair at a time, place opposite emotions at either end of the room, e.g. happy and upset, etc. Get each person to walk towards the feeling which best describes the Blobs on their card. If they really can't decide, then they could remain in the middle of the room. When they have moved, each person could share their picture with someone nearby to see if they would agree. We've learned that **motion stirs e-motions**.

2 Place four emotion cards on a table which contain negative Blob feelings. Ask the group to select the most negative card they would choose to remove from the group and explain why. Continue removing them until there is only one Blob left. Who has the most positive feelings on the card?

3 In a one-to-one situation, split the pack, then both find a Blob from within each group that represents how you felt when you were a child, a teenager, an adult, and now. Start by sharing your thoughts to model how to do it.

4 Large group – enlarge three cards on an A3 sheet on the photocopier, leaving space for writing around each image. Divide your group into smaller groups of about sic. Each group should be given the same images to discuss. The question could focus upon trying to work out why each of the characters feels the way they do in each picture. In turn, get the group's feedback on their ideas on the different characters.

5 Small groups – place a set of emotion cards on the table. Ask the group to put them into an order which provides a story. The process should be focused not so much upon finding the 'right story' but on creating one together as a group.

6 One-to-one – draw a line on a piece of paper so that the page is divided in half. Take one card at a time and decide whether the Blob is a positive feeling overall or a negative one. After sorting a set number, decide if there are any you would like to change. You may need to take the initiative and suggest a change.

DOI: 10.4324/9781003456551-9

7 Large group – pass out an emotion card to each person/pair. Get them to write a short prayer for one of the characters who they feel has the greatest needs. To make it more personal, they might like to imagine them as someone they know without mentioning them by name, only feelings.

8 Small group – place a cut-out heart in the middle of the table. Choose each card in turn, and decide how easy it would be to love someone feeling like this Blob. Groups may disagree about this. It is not how much we choose to love the Blobs but how easy/hard it is to love the feelings being expressed.

9 One-to-one – take the pack and shuffle it. Cut the pack and discuss a friend who sometimes feels like one of the Blobs on the cards and why. Move to describing ourselves when trust is built up. You could move deeper by selecting specific individuals we know, e.g. brothers, sisters, relatives, dad and mum.

10 Large group – get each group to act out their own emotion card Blobs with the others around them. You might like them to do this using only body language, no words. Halt the drama every few seconds to describe your observations. Only do this with a group who you trust can manage this (and whom you can manage!).

11 Small group – take six Blobs and imagine they were the same Blob at different times of the day. Discuss which emotions are definitely more likely to occur in the morning, at lunchtime, afternoons, at the end of school/work, in the evening, and just before sleep.

12 One-to-one: find a Blob emotions card which has a feeling that is behaving most like your friend, your mum, your dad, or yourself. Discuss each one openly as they are identified. They may be on one card or several.

13 Large group – place a card on a large piece of paper and leave it on a wall for a day. Invite people to write their feelings on the sheet to explain why the Blob is as it is. Encourage people to add to other comments. It could be done as an activity with several sheets around the room and people rotating.

14 Small group – take random pairs of cards from the pack. As a group, try to suggest what happened after the first card to create the picture on the second. This could be repeated a few times.

15 One-to-one – place five cards in front of you. Turn the Blobs over that you agree have only negative feelings. The aim of this activity is to agree. Then discuss the positive feelings. You may uncover people's deep-seated fears, so be prepared for unusual answers.

16 Large group – hold up a card with a set of Blobs on it. Go around the circle saying something that each Blob might say in a day. Model this a few times.

17 Small group – give an emotion card to each person in the group without anyone else seeing it. Then take back the cards, shuffle them up and lay them on the table for all to see. One by one, take turns to answer questions about your card. Your answers should describe the feelings of the character. See if the group can identify which is your Blob emotion card.

All of the above ideas can be adapted for the different dynamics of group size, making 50 ideas in total! There are many more that you can do with Blob cards. Let us know which ones work for you. Happy blobbing!

SUPPORT MATERIAL

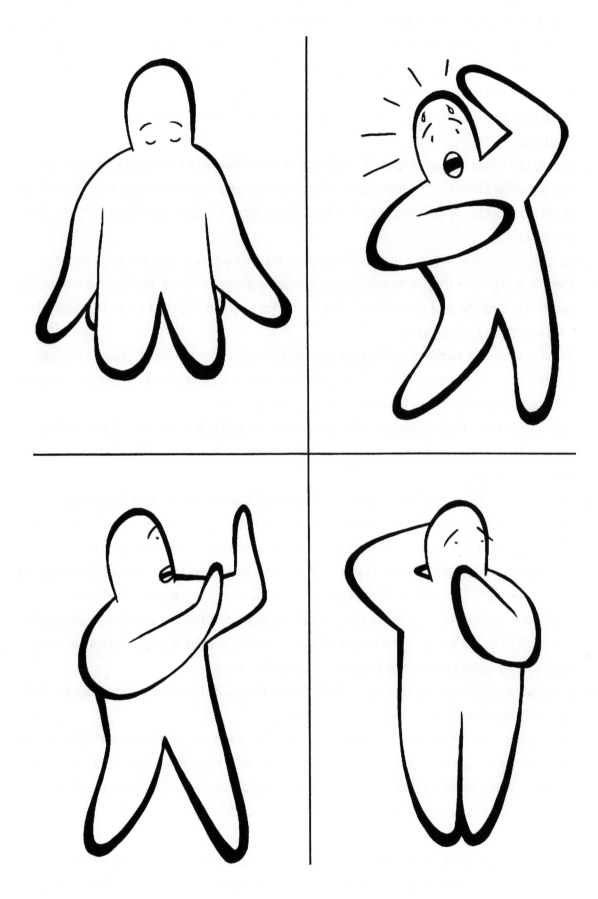

Copyright material from Pip Wilson and Ian Long (2024), *My Blob Feelings Workbook*, Routledge

Copyright material from Pip Wilson and Ian Long (2024), *My Blob Feelings Workbook*, Routledge

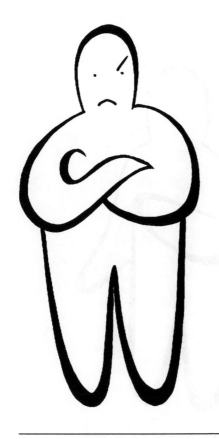

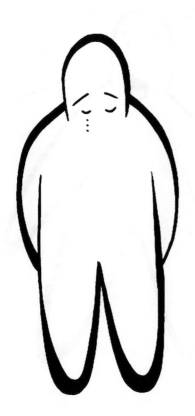

Copyright material from Pip Wilson and Ian Long (2024), *My Blob Feelings Workbook*, Routledge

Copyright material from Pip Wilson and Ian Long (2024), *My Blob Feelings Workbook*, Routledge

Copyright material from Pip Wilson and Ian Long (2024), *My Blob Feelings Workbook*, Routledge

Copyright material from Pip Wilson and Ian Long (2024), *My Blob Feelings Workbook*, Routledge

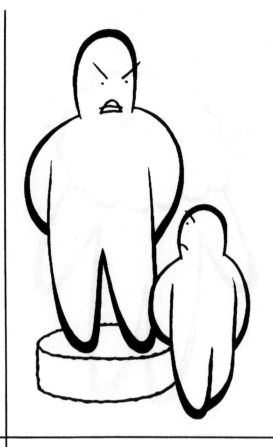

Copyright material from Pip Wilson and Ian Long (2024), *My Blob Feelings Workbook*, Routledge

*For Product Safety Concerns and Information please contact
our EU representative GPSR@taylorandfrancis.com Taylor & Francis
Verlag GmbH, Kaufingerstraße 24, 80331 München, Germany*

T - #0089 - 090625 - C0 - 297/210/6 - SB - 9781032598444 - Matt Lamination